Also by SJ Blasko:

Midnight Comes

Losing the Stars
The Library & Her Keeper (coming soon)

Anthology works:
Space Kitties: Feline Forays Through the Galaxies
There is Us (coming June 2020)

the flowers

need Love

The flowers need love to grow too

to grow too ♡

Dedications

Thank you. Thank you, thank you, thank you.
My dear friends: Marci. Adrien. Emily. Bobby.
Brad. Mackenzie.
Hannah. Rachael. Sarah.
Polly. Emily. Blu.
Mary. Jack.
Bekah. Lizzy. Anna.
Ezra. Elsa. Trey.
Rae and Raechel.
I cannot. Words cannot.

I have so much love in my heart for you all.
You fight me, teach me, love me, hound me, help me, lift
me, remind me to bloom.

I love you, I love you, I love you.

someday i'll regret all the
things i do not say

but for now it is the only
way i know

(to keep
me safe)

Introduction

One April
I learned my love for poetry
But then
I had nothing to say

So, I wrote about fairytales
Because I didn't know yet
How to write the poetry
Of me

Now,
Poetry spills from my fingers
Like spaghetti
The noodles run deeper than you think
And it is not always possible to separate them

Like a glass too full
I am too full
Stacked symbols in a trench coat
Passing for innocuous.
Fragments,
Held on the brink of falling
Saved
By surface tension.

ONE:

The flowers need water to grow.

Yes… And?

And love.

The flowers need love to grow too.

TWO:

the first flight

I stand on the precipice.
It is me, and the world.
The horizon is my boundary,
And the distance between stretches so long
I hardly expect to reach it.

Excitement swells

                    I leap—

On a blustery day in February

We walked beside busy streets,
Four friends, sharing Saturday.
The wind blew around us,
over us and through us
From every direction
pulling hair, and clothes, and words.

The coffee shop behind us
had been warm, with wi-fi,
four-tables in corners
where we sat together.
Three friends and a sibling.
And ahead was McDonald's
where our faces could thaw
while we stuffed them with fries.

And between stretched the sidewalks
Short cuts, long cuts, sure cuts, lost cuts.
Laughing and talking,
we gripped warm drinks in cold hands
And time lifted its burden;
Stayed for us, delayed for us,
waited at our pace
for the three siblings and a friend
Who'd found each other
across its vast expanse.

14

*ill take No supper tonight,
please.*

> *I'll take no supper tonight, please.*
> *I've taken my fill of the world.*
> *I've quenched my thirst on the dews of the earth*
> *and the breeze as it whispers and whorls.*

Reflections

Reflections are tricky things.
Man didn't create them
Only trapped them
Hung them on a wall for his own vain glory.
The glassy stillness of a lake
Was first
To echo reality above it.
Distorted,
It ripples like a gateway
At the kiss of a stone.

It calls, it beckons
I have mystery lurking
And what will happen if you,
Little you,
Dare to pass through
With no intention of return?
One might find oneself upside down
Standing in the sky
And brushing ones feet against the stars.
Or there might be monsters
Real ones
Which we can touch and feel and fight
And see while fighting
As the seeds of monstrous things
Separate themselves from us

In the last few seconds of life
And we see them laid out

Even knowing this,
The water calls
To the nine tenths of us it possesses
Enticing us
With the idea of a world
Identical to ours.
(we think)
Have you ever stopped,
Looked,
Counted the branches?
It would be impossible,
So we assume.

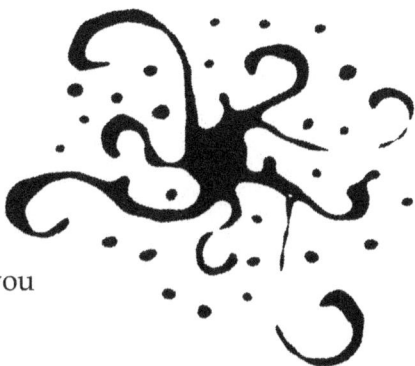

And as the water accepts you
(Feet,
Waist,
Hands,
Shoulders,
Hair, drifting like seaweed in the tide)
It whispers to you
Just a little deeper now

So you go on,
On,
On until you discover, or drown

Or,
Until you are pulled upwards
By arms grasping you around the chest
As your lungs burn with the ache of tipped scales,
The balance within you lost
And you hear the voice whisper,
Breath warming your ear:

(Not like this
My friend
Not like this.)

yellow-lit cabin

There were eight of us
In the yellow-lit cabin
With the Christmas lights on the wall.
We chatted as we crammed
Clothes into suitcases and bags
Words into paragraphs.
Years into a night.
I wanted to stay forever
    (and then some)

There was a huge, brown moth
On the door
And someone let it in
Causing shrieking
And scrambling for top bunks.
Lucy killed it.
And we packed in enforced quiet after that.

Then, there was only I and the counselor
In the hollow cabin
With the sunlight streaming in.
The screen door was propped open
And the breeze drifted through
Snaking through the empty spaces
And over the neatly made beds.
We were quiet
Nothing left to say,
And all I wanted to do
Was leave.

19

Cats

Time is like a cat:
Regal,
Bad-tempered,
Moody like the swing of the summer wind.
It rips and tears and weeps and shelters
And I soar on its currents
Up drafts
Down drafts
As I draft
Poetry inspired by the howling gales.

The muse is also like a cat.
It loves to be stroked and petted
Rubbed behind the ears.
But whether or not
It decides *you* are worthy
To touch its head
Run your fingers across its fur-
Whether it grants you
A sandpaper lick on your fingers
Or curls its tail around your wrist
Or, heaven bless you, purrs,
Is the challenge.

But maybe that's the way of it.
The way that growing up goes.
As we put off our childish fantasies,
Drowned out by the woes of the world.

the first flight

I stood on the precipice.
It was me, and the world
And the horizon was my boundary
(one so far
I never planned to reach it.)

Excitement swelled

I leapt

(I fell)

THREE:

the free fall

be gentle, ever with yourself

Have you ever lain
On a hardwood floor
As the breeze of a fan skated
Over the dip and curve of your back,
Tracing the skin which
You allow no one to touch?
(you,
     even you avoid
                    fixing your attention there)
Have you ever drawn in
And let out a breath
Just to prove you could?
To listen to this thing,
This process, this care which is
Keeping you alive?
(remember when
you were a child
and you were scared
that the thickness in your throat
would suffocate you?
remember how you first sat
on this same floor
with the dresser drawers pulled out
next to you
and learned to quell panic attacks
by remembering to breathe
even when you were scared you couldn't?)

It didn't occur to you

(it never did)

To ask for help.
You thought that growing up
And learning to be human
Had to be done on one's own.
You were so desperate to be normal,
And yet, like portents and omens
You were always afraid
of a mutiny within

(rather than
harm from any external source.)

Darling,
You were a child.
You had never grown up human before.
How did you think
You could teach yourself
Everything you didn't know?
Even now, you try.
        Remember, dearheart, please—
                Be gentle, even with yourself.

Weather Report

Cloudy today
The weatherman would say
Of me
Of my mind
Clouded haze
Foggy thoughts
Like wading through the humid day
When
It's *supposed* to rain
From all accounts
But the clouds
Are huffy
And say
They'll take the 12%
Chance of a light breeze from the northwest
Chance of seeing someone you like
Chance of meatballs
For dinner
(for eight hundred, Alex)

It might clear up tomorrow
He'd continue,
Scratching an itch on his neck
Smiling for the cameras
Because there are people watching
Always watching
And they rely
On the weatherman

To predict
To announce
To call
With accuracy

It might
He says again, looking less certain
With every word
It might

It might be sunny, with bright
Wisps of white
Glossing across the cerulean sky —
Wouldn't that be nice?
And a warm
Breeze
And
Who knows,
Really?
After all,
There must be showers
Before the roses bloom.
After all,
He repeats
Looking to the left
Stage right
Where the rain
Is not planning to fall
Not yet

Not today
Not yet.

And the whole
The whole of it
Whole comedic
Scene is trapped
In limbo
(like the space
before a bathroom
where there is no bathroom
sink or mirror
too sheltered to loiter
too exposed to cry
which serves no purpose
in the grand scheme)
In my mind

But that's all there is sometimes
Cloud
Haze
Fog
With the promise
Of sunshine
Tomorrow

(Or just
tomorrow)

First Law of Motion

First Law of Motion:
An object in motion
Will remain in motion

And today I am glad
Because even hurtling
Through space and time
At dizzying speeds
Through blinding oceans
Of stars and rings of planets
And meteors and comets
(I always seem to dodge
Last second)

Even then
I know that
If I keep
Moving
Forward
I will not
buckle,
       crumble,
             collapse.

*(Because an object at rest
may never move again.)*

okay

You said I was okay
I said I was, okay?
They heard (that) I was okay

A funny order, it is.

I believed you
When you told me
That I was okay
When you were not in my shoes
and neither were They

But when
I said I was not okay
You asked if I was sure.
Sure it would not pass?
(because okay, is default?)
and they heard you, not me.

So
Am I sure it won't pass?
No
I am certain it will
Because everything does.
What doesn't kill me
Makes me stronger

(But

it

n e e d s

n o t

to

k i l l

me)

7:24 am

The grass is dead
And frozen solid.
It is hard and brittle like shale
Cracking beneath my feet
Lumps and dips and valleys
petrified under me.
I am alive
But even my breath turns granite grey,
Heavy in the marble air.
And I think
Maybe
The whole world
By unanimous decision
Is stone today
And I overslept
Rushing,
Missed the memo
Some cosmic sticky note
Etched in the corner of my eye:
A Reminder that Today
We are Collectively Asleep.
But the Words bubble up inside of me
Those big Words
With the space of galaxies between them

Like continents
Each word
is an island.

Tapped into the spring of the universe,
I draw from the wealth
of our million words unsaid.
Stone?
Stone is dead.
I hear
I see
I breathe
I feel
I am
too much to be stone.
So on I walk
The only living thing in a mausoleum
With a burning heart
To stave off the welcoming void.

Lost

There are some people who speak in blobs
Text clouds of most used words
Until the meaning is lost
In the traditional

Like reaching a hand into water so murky
Your fingers all but disappear,
And trying to pull out
A string of slime.

This is not intuition
This is impression
(Un-intention):
Emphasis upon inflection
Ends up in in-distinction
And I am lost
To introspection.

someday

Someday I'll regret
All the things I do not say
But for now
It is the only way I know
(To keep me safe.)

DANGEROUS

I am fascinated by the fire.
I could sit and watch its dance
Sit and listen to the snap-crackle song of it
For hours

Something in it calls to me
In the dark places of my heart.
Maybe that is why I stay
So far away—

Because if I let it
It will take hold of my hand
Crawl its fingers up my arm
And lodge its heat in my soul

Like the sliver of ice
And the poisoned kiss
That drove Kai to forget
His love
His home
His name
I may forget
That I am not fire too.

If I let it,
It will set me ablaze
And I will not stop
Until coals and ashes
Stain my feet
And the whole world burns
Around me.

Unstitched

Unstitched is a melancholy word
The kind that tastes like apple
Like sharp snow mountains
And curving swelling dives
Like blue-green ink
The color of sea dragon scales
Across a page of lines
Waiting to be filled and set on a shelf
Untouched, as the pages curl
And the spiral rusts.
Around it, the world keeps turning
Around and around.
But it is not part of it
Because it is too delicate now
To be lived with; to be loved
Any more than from afar
Until it wishes it was never filled
Never used, and never used up, thusly
And it envies the unstitched
All that was sown and unsewn
Before it could grow old.
It envies the possibilities
For that is its purpose
A notebook
To take note of possibilities
But what is the worth?
Who will listen, read, write, at risk of damage?

Do you know how easily paper,

words,

can
ignite?

fire

Funny.
They all turn round to fire in the end.
It snakes its way through everything
Everything I write.
I wonder why.
Circles don't seem
Complicated enough.
I want a ball of string to untangle
A knot of necklace laces
An infinite puzzle
In which I seek occupation
(Not revelation.)

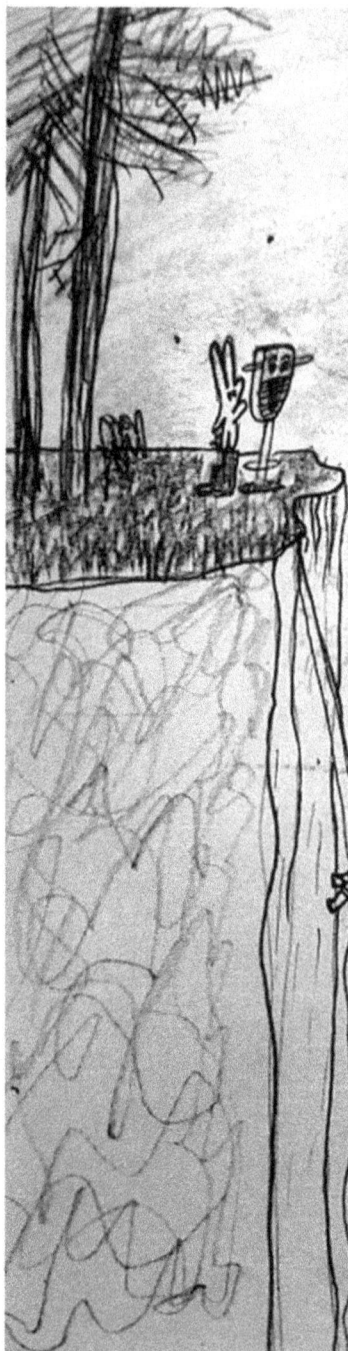

i hope even now,
they are going
all the places we used to
dream of

because,
i am going places too

good places
happy places

(it just took time
and their somedays

came sooner
than mine)

-sj blaska

oh the places you'll go...

When I was younger
I had a card
(two)
Hanging on the wall.
Above the lamp
On the purple table
Beside my bed.
They were more trapezoidal
Than rectangular
And they both said the same thing:

"Oh,
    The places you'll go!"

I don't know where they are now.
I lost track of them
On the day I tore down all the posters
In a fit of—
Well,
Something that quickly passed.
Like a rainstorm
Over by the time
you've rushed to the window to see it.
The next time I entered
That stark, slanted wall
Moved me to tears

(I thought
I thought
I thought that
In order to grow
I had to strip myself of everything I held close.

I fell
Into the trap of believing
That childish things
Were those things
One loved as a child.

I stripped myself bare
Like the wall
And like the wall
The starkness cut deep.)

Anyway.
I don't know what happened to them
To the cards.
I hope—

I hope
They were recycled.
That even now
They are going
All the places we dreamed of going.

I hope they are.

(because I am going places too.
Good places
Happy places.
I just took a while
And their somedays
Came sooner than mine)

FOUR:

the figuring

Law of Motion
(the second)

I used to be well.

I did.
I think.
But it's been years,
Years,
Years
When I was not

And I don't remember
quite
What being well
is like.

I mean-
I mean-
I mean-
I am always well.
I am
Always moving.
Because an object at rest-

I've said this already.

So I'll rest when I'm dead
Or I'll die when I rest

And I'm not ready
yet
I haven't made my mark
yet
I haven't swelled my voice
With the chorus of those
who came before me
(yet)
I haven't heard that note
One note
In a symphony
The glorious harmony
I haven't drawn a breath
And heard the empty space
And felt the sharp prick of awe
That the gap
Is for me to fill.
Little gap,
Little me.

And that,
I think,
Holds me here.
Roots my feet to the ground
To Earth.
Because humans
Are delicate.
It would not take much
To flee this mortal form

But
I am not ready
It is not my time
I am secure
Knowing my days are numbered
Measured out
By One
Who does not lose count
Lose thought
Think
All in the wrong order
At all the times
Which are
Most inopportune.

It is my greatest honor
(It is my greatest humbling)

And anyways
I am, well,
Well enough to sing,
To dance.
Well enough for joy
To light its fire
Bursting pyrotechnics
In my chest

(Except
Of course
When I am not.
Not when my thoughts
Take the wheel
And I am caught in loops
Loops
Loops)

"Shape without form
Shade without color"
I drift
In monochromatic waves
Clinging to the memory
And hope of hues
Beyond my mind's walls.
I drift
In soft piano melodies
And synesthesia winds my senses
In a great tangle
Melancholy tastes like apple
But un-anchored
Only smells like dust
Looping and twirling in the breeze
Over the ocean
Invisible
Under the too-wide sky
Over the too-bright sea.

Until it hits city
And the city
Brings it back down,
Tearing it
Into a million
Tiny
Fragments

(They used to be it
They used to be whole
They were once
But now
Not)

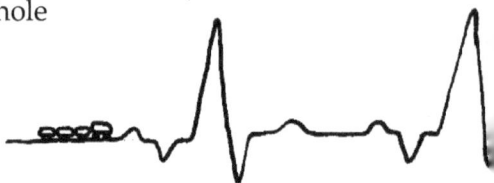

And just like that
The conclusion
Brings me down
With a jolt and a bump and a thud
Like a plane
Or the clanking chains
Of a rollercoaster

My stomach is doing rollercoaster loops
Loops
Loops
I used to be well-
(i've said that too)
-but sometimes
I am well now

And I forget
That with a breath
I can be
Not.

It is terrifying
But I am not always scared
You know,
Part of life
Is living it.

*This was supposed to be
More coherent.*

Little fish in a big water.
Little girl in a big world.
And though I exist beneath the surface
I only hope my tail leaves ripples on the
topside too.

little fish

Night Skies & Autumn Fires

Do you believe in wishes?
I don't.

But when the air is crisp
As a shriveled leaf
And the simple act
Of moving through space
Is loud
When every breath is seen
As well as felt
And the wind
Whispers up a whirlwind
Of fallen soldiers
Who clung valiantly to their branches
From Spring
To the Fall
And the cold feels
So
So
Alive

Then, I might.

When there is a gathering of friends
Forged in the innocence of youth
Strengthened in the flames of time

And when the chill is driven back
By mankind's oldest light
And when there is warmth
At my face
Cold
At my back
And a stitch in my side
Where joy, and light,
And normalcy
(with just a hint
of the Potentially Extraordinary)
have begun to sew back together
the tear
left by the thorn

then, I might.

When we walk
Along darkened hometown streets
When our laughter reaches the stars
When the darkness swirls
And gathers around us
But we do not mind
Because we are alive
And aglow
And achingly, presently, here

Then, I might.

I might believe in wishes
Because all of mine
Have come true.

The road

Make a wish on the road.
Press a palm flat on the pavement
Dig the tips of your fingers
Into dark, gritty, speckled asphalt
(or whatever it is,
                            this stuff that roads are made from)
Memorize every dip and divot.
Impossible, isn't it?
Now slip your wish inside one
One crack in a zillion
And let anonymity keep it safe.

Now lift your hand, your head.
The road is your horizon
Your path to anywhere
(your raging river,
holding you in.)
(your border walls;
your boundary.)
It carries us to work,
School,
To church,
Sometimes.
Where else do we need to go?

The road…

        The road…

The road
And those who travel on it
with no deviation
have imitated to perfection and beyond—
Aye, further:
      to replacement
of the dreamers and their stars

why should we not wish on it?
        they demand,
            it is something we can touch.

They miss the part
Where we learn it
Its flaws and crystal facets
And that is why we call it beautiful
And entrust that it will safely store our dreams
Until we can return for them.

i would not be afraid

Give me a screen
A blank document
A field of snow;

I would not be afraid.

I would trample my footprints;
Leave my mark.

I would not be afraid.
Not today.

Because today, I am as empty
As the text box;
As the screen.

And it would be a relief
To see a mark:
Visible
And left by my hand.

It would mean I have not lost my voice.

Focus on the color...

"Focus on the color"

The color... of what?
Everything is colors
I can count the exceptions
Not the multitude
Everything is colors
Because somewhere in creation
My wires were crossed
Everything is colors
The way my stomach growls and writhes
Like a thing alive
The black of my boots against the seat of this chair
The way you look at me.
The music playing over the speakers
It would be simpler
If you asked me to focus on the void
A few colorless forms
The way my mind drains of all but fuzz
Or the air that whistles through me
The words of a novel too easy to read, too hard to
comprehend
The way I look at you.

late bloomer

Don't call me a late bloomer
Don't imply to me
And everyone else
That there was a mark
That I missed it
Because bold of you to assume
I have not already bloomed
That I have not blossomed beautifully
Just because
I prefer leaves to flowers
And grew into my tree
Instead of your rose.

Don't call me a late bloomer
Don't imply to me
And everyone else
That there was a mark
That I missed it
Because bold of you to assume
I have not already bloomed
That I have not blossomed beautifully
Just because
I prefer leaves to flowers
And grew into my tree
Instead of your rose

LISTEN.

I dreamt a dream last night.
They've been coming more of late.
And frankly, though my eyelids weigh,
I am afraid to go to sleep.

I dreamed of kisses
A partner overcome by passion
Who could not
At my beauty
Hold back.
(to be fair to him,
this imaginary man,
it was the beauty of my soul
not attraction to this mortal form-
or so he said)
(to be fair to me,
I told him no.
and he took my consent
danced it like a coin
between his fingers
and with a magician's trick
he made it disappear.)
Because he was so in love with me.

Sir.
If you loved me,
You would listen.

I

placed

my

growth

on

becoming

(a difficult task)

i can breathe

There is so much world
And so little me.
I find myself in stories
And in silence
In the birdsong
That fills the space between thoughts.

I've read once
        Twice
               A million times
That geniuses have messy handwriting—
All of them.
That sloppy penmanship,
Though not art to be looked at
or admired,
Is a sign of a busy mind.
Your thoughts raced your hand
And won.

Perhaps that is why cursive has become my saving
grace
The letters are allowed to blend together
Blurring lines in touch-starved intimacy.
In an ever going, ever growing train
Of loops and curves
And it is allowed to be called beautiful.

The blank field of page
Is quiet behind them
And in the space
Between each knotted curl of string
Is the silence

And in the silence

I can breathe.

Don't write me poetry

Don't write me poetry
It's never worked before
Vanity, all of it, vanity
And I don't want any
More-words, just-words, nothing-but words.

I don't care for the structure
The way it is so easy to steal
Phrases, lines
Automatic sigh-bringers
Used a thousand times
By history's pen
And those more worthy to hold it than you

All you did
Was take the bag
Of scrabble tiles
Rattling and clacking together
And shake
Once
Twice
Thrice
Forced
Farce
Until you were satisfied with the tiles it gave
And you threw away the rest—

That's not art
That's strategy.

It's too neat.
Neat like summer,
Neat like children's books
(not the good kind)
Formula following
Empty and hollow-ringing.

Give me something real
Instead.
Give me the ramblings, twisting
wanderings of your mind
give me the dark places
the secrets
the beauties and joys
and mysteries that lurk in the depths
like sea dragons
like the ocean itself
there is so much more
so much wilder and deeper

so

grab my hand
and pull me in with you

don't flatter me while dipping our toes.
because why,
why would we choose the ship—
safe little dingy
bleached wood, branded logo on the side
—when underneath
lies Atlantis
and
the depths?

(so
don't write me poetry
don't write poetry
for me.
write the poetry of you,
and trust me enough
to share it.)

Dear younger me.

Dear Younger Me.
The days ahead are dark.

There will be points
Where you will close your eyes
Burning, stinging, tear-torn eyes
And it will look no brighter
When you open them again.
You will reach for the light switch
Only to discover
The dual bulbs
Clustered under the shade
Are doing all they can already.
You will walk upstairs
In the witching hour
The dark scary still hour
And even though there is nothing
Nothing logical to fear
The still scary dark hour
And the night will surround you
Press in on you
And you'll swear each step is a mouth
Waiting to swallow you alive.
You will leap from light switch to light switch
Because the dark

The cursed, smothering dark
Is a fate worse
Than sinking into a molten floor.

Dear Younger Me.

The darkness does not win,
Not against the light.
Remember that.

Even if you, yourself, don't feel light.
Even when you feel bogged down
Like the weight of a thousand worlds
Rests on your shoulders
And you're slogging through swamp mud besides.
There is light, and hope, and peace
Peace like none you have ever known
Waiting on the other side.
And if I could spare you the tears
The ache that tears your chest inside out
The lump that threatens to stay
Choking you
Breath by breath
Forever
If I could spare you that—
But you would never grow.
You would never become me.
Broken. Imperfect. Beautiful.
Stronger, holding tight to your Savior's hand.
I wouldn't trade all the stars to be you again, me.
But someday you'll get here. April 2018.
You'll write a poem. Me to you.
Heart to heart.
You'll look around. You'll look back.
And there will be light again.

See you when you get here, yeah?

FIVE:

the fear

I am back
Standing on the precipice
Ready to fly
                    (I think)
And yet
Not ready to leap
                    (tell me, is there any other way?)

I am afraid
And the fear rises
And the excitement mutes.
The horizon suddenly
Seems too far
when I am too afraid to leave this branch,
And the boundary is laughable.
I will never reach it
if I do not first conquer the ones within.

Mayday

M a y d a y
M a y d a y
Is   my   cry
If   I   sink
Into this sea
Of h a p p y
(Maybe) happy
M a y d a y
M a y d a y
I   may forget
How   to carry
The   weight
Of   s   a   d.

Turn to the light
    (my shadow is long...)

Come,
            You say
            and hold out your hands
Come,
Into the light.

And I am coming
            But slowly
Because there is something
So
    So
            Dangerous
In the light
For in the light
Shadows shrivel up and die
(and I am tied to the way
mine dances behind me)

I hardly notice it
(though,
        sometimes,
                it drags heavily on me)

What luggage,
As we travel through life
We pull on silent wheels behind.

Come
      You say
            And I worry
that you are annoyed,
               impatient,
with me.

But I have grown
Accustomed to the weight behind me

      (is it truly weight
            if we do not notice?
      we do not consider,
           for example
                  our arms,
                 our heads,
                our feet
            to be heavy.)

Imagine a world without shadow?

I can,
        I think
And in my mind,
        it is bright
        and glorious.
No shadow,
        because there is nothing except light

(and I am reminded
                        again)

Come into the light
        You say

But
I
Am
Scared
because
there
is
no shadow
        without light
and in the dark
        there is no weight

(No more than the air in our lungs
        is weight
           when there is air all around us as well)

(in space
              would be a different matter)

I am scared of the light.
      Even as my stanzas trail
      off
           away
                from
                        it

They trail behind my pen in ribbons of ink
Like my shadow trails behind my hand
Slicing the page it passes across

I
Am
Afraid
Because
The
Light
Cuts

Deep
And
The
Shadow
Trails
Long
And
It
   Is
      Interesting
         To me
            That a shadow
               Is made from
               Anything
            That is
               Too
                  Dense
                     For the light
                        To pass
                  Through

(and therefore
         I am scared
         to learn just
            how
                        long
               mine
                  may
                     be)

(I forget:
"the light shines in the darkness,
and the darkness *has not overcome it*.")

so come

     you say
  turn to the light
     and I respond

                  i respond

Leaf (i.)

I did not let go in a shower
butterfly wings and
golden sundrops
Not in a cloud
where the rattling of the descent
sent soft rustles and
shivers rippling through the
child watching
Wide eyes
bright mind
purest confetti
for the party of one
 (a coming of age)

no,
i let go
little
and late

                                        (and alone.)

(don't give me your heart)

Don't give me your heart—
What if I break it?
Don't give me your love
What if I can't return it?
Don't give me your trust
What if I drop it?

What if it slips?
The fragile thing
You've placed in my hands
Slips through my
Fumbling
Shaking
Fingers
The clumsy ones
That are more used to shambling across a keyboard
In a complicated dance of the mind
Than brushing aside
Loose locks of hair
(your hair)

Matters of the heart
Those are breakable.

And I don't know what to say

To these things
These heart stopping
Breath dropping
Beautiful things
I blush and I hide and I steady my breathing
because
What can I say but
No?

I'm not
Not special
Not amazing
Or anything
Of the kind.
(kind
I try to be kind.
Shouldn't everybody?)
But what if
What if
What if you saw
What lies in my mind
Not that I am a lie
I promised once
I will not lie
Not to you
Not about you
Not for you
But that there is more
More darkness

I am not a companion
Nursing wounds
Bringing cheer
Brightening the days
I am the doctor
Busy
So busy
Fixing the world
Holding shattered fragments
All the lives of ever and to be
In my hands
And I forget
How easy it is to forget
That I
Am not
Self sufficient
And
That the lemon
chocolate
black tea words
You give so freely
Might be true
Of me

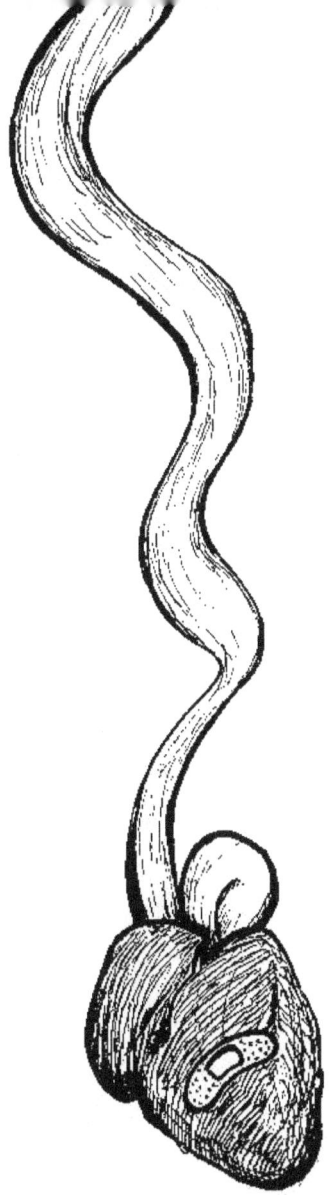

of me too.

drowned rat.

Heart chesting
Pound pounding
Words muddled unsaid
People talking
Self knotting
In circles and loops inside my head
Worried that the
Words will be
Wrong and wrong and right
Outnumbered by
The errors of
The fact that I am me

I go back
I reread
There is more space in my head now
To breathe
Not breathe
More than breathe
I can speak.

And then the flood again
And I am like a mouse on a sinking ship
Bailing with a thimble

As it is all my tiny hands can fit around
Dwarfed by the rushing waterfall
Leaks
From the ocean
Of
Stuff
Out there
So big

And I pause
And cock my head
Whiskers quivering
Tail sodden and submerged
As the waters rise
And I find my peace
Among the rising flood

And all of this was stupid
Maybe
Words I'll never show
To anybody

But fun
For that
Four stanzas
Like a drowned rat.

SIX:

the second flight

breath-taking

I find my space in the silence
In the cool dappled shadow of a tree
Beneath a glowing canopy
Under a blue sky
In the heavy-laden damp air
Where a glistening gem
Of a droplet might form
At any second
Suspended
(like the noise in my mind)
The result?
Breath taking.

Leaf (ii)

This is my tree
And I have been safe all my life
Spring through golden Summer

But now
The air cools
And the wind gusts
And I
watch
As we all fall

First
I am an observer only
I do not understand
But then
The cold sliver of age
Loosens my grip on the tree
My tree
          my life
(because I am not enough
without my tree)

I hold on tighter
I hold on
For a long time
(probably too long)

Until "safe"
      Becomes scared
Until I look down
And see that i
Am not the same colors
Orange and red and gold
Burn through my beautiful
Safe
Green

    I hate them.

And I let go
Not by choice
But by necessity
Torn from a branch in the middle of a storm
Thrown
      Tossed
         In a flurry
From one wind to the next
Until I land
In a pile of my fallen brethren
One in a million
      (one of a million)
And the rain beats down
And the sunlight pours
And I sink into the earth
And hope I will be braver when I rise.

beautiful

it means so much
that someone like you
you, who finds everyone
beautiful
think that I am beautiful
(too)

the One who lives

"Scabulous. Adjective.
Proud of a scar on your body,
which is an autograph
signed to you by a world
grateful for your continued willingness to play
with her,
even when you don't feel like it."
-The Dictionary of Obscure Sorrows

I am not afraid of scars;
They mean that I have chanced to live.

They mean that I have seen the world,
And the world has seen me.
That we have locked our gaze
Our eyes
Our wills in battle
Mortal combat
And it has blinked first.

They mean that I am a warrior.
They mean that I am a survivor.

They mean that I have healed,
Because scars come after wounds.
After we stitch closed
Our rips, and tears, and holes,
Patching ourselves up
Holding close our precious blood.

(Because a scar that still hurts
Means a fight unfinished.)

They are a warning.
They are a story.
They are a reminder.
Of love, and loss,
And life,
Beautiful life.

The moment when you catch a glimpse of death
Out of the corner of your eye.
And it sees you
And it nods
And you know it will come back
Someday
To collect.
But not today.
Because today
Today, you are the one who lives;

tale as old as time . . .

It is remarkable and strange
At curtain close
That this is truly
"the end"

Because yes
All of life's a stage
And we are all the players

But this story
This tale as old as time
Which has happened
Nine times
Like clockwork
Will never again be told
Here
Like this

And it really makes one think
About the fleeting
And the forever.

SEVEN:

hello roaring monster

hello roaring monster
screaming beast
i've missed you.
the way you put me in perspective
you are my war,
and i am my champion.
you are my dragon,
and i am the princess
who slays you herself.

but not yet

because if I slay you
I must return,
go back to my kingdom
(or not,
and break my family's hearts)
and i am not ready for that.

I have been gone for so long
what if the kingdom has moved on
without me?

and
besides
I understand this dragon
but what if once i am free
another comes?
to learn to be held prisoner
                           again
                 by another
would destroy me.

so what is free?
I have tamed my dragon;
learned to live.

is it not enough?
No.
i want it dead.
dead and gone and buried.

the war cries in my ears
and crescents bleed from my palms.
a scream builds in my throat

i cannot kill it
because with familiar comes safe

                    *(and Lord and stars and skies
                        i just want to be safe.)*

EIGHT:

the third f(l)ight

How many?
How many times can I fall?
How many before I will attempt this flight no more?

The answer?

(As many as I have
and one more, always)

cerebral thunderstorm

This cerebral thunderstorm is raging strong tonight
Celestial stars, swirling cosmos,
colors and nebula
Lightning and wind and rain and noise
White noise
Not to dampen and smother
But to wash away
All but what matters
And leave only pellucid calm
After the storm has passed.

heartache

It feels like heartache
To remember
That there is snow above the clouds
Which melts
Before it ever touches earth

drowning

Why do people hate the rain?

Why do people
        h   a   t   e
                        anything?

Why expel that effort,
When instead
You could just let it roll
off your back
        over your head
                into your lungs?

but wait—
that is called
d   r   o   w   n   i   n   g

                        (my mistake)

dichotomy

Such a beautiful dichotomy
To see the clouds part
For just a second
As the sun illuminates
A downpour of diamonds.

eye of the storm

When I set out
The air was chilled
And stirring restlessly
(and so was I).
When I walked farther
The air had calmed
And raindrops sprinkled down
Like thoughts
(light, like my mind).
And now
As I sit
The heavens loose their load;
Water pours down the road
In the gully between street and sidewalk.

I am chilled to the bone
And sirens wail
As a firetruck rushes by
In paralleled tandem with
The thunder
And the train
And a second truck
What irony—
Bitter, ashy on the tongue
—That anything could burn
Against this deluge.

I couldn't.

If I were out there, I would plant my feet
Spread my arms
Tip my face to the sky
And let the grey swallow me
And the wind envelop me
And the water pour into me
Filling all the hollow spaces
Until I drown
Or worse,
I learn to breathe the water
Silently
In the calm of the heart
At the eye of the storm.

flood

The rain pools
And fills up
All the crevices of my mind
And bits and scraps of words
Float to me on the water

But then the rain stops
And the flood recedes
And all I am left with
Are wads of paper mâché-d words
And a little less clutter
Than I was storing before.

white noise

Outside
Rain like snow is falling
And despite old stains
Leaks immortalized on the ceiling
The inside is warm and aglow
Graced
By the pleasant chatter
Of strangers
And friends
As mixed music plays
And machines whir
Stirring scents of sugar and spice
Coffees and confections
Hang in the air

Lukewarm chai lingers on my tongue
And the etch of my pen
Is muted
        (almost, but not quite)

This
This is the white noise
Which stories are born of.

this time

I find

Peace
          In the
Pieces
          Of the
Poems
          I
Pen

By this window
Of this room
In this time.

I want to write poetry
But I don't have words.
I want to write novels
But they are so long.
I want to make people
            f e e l things
But I
            like a hypocrite
Am an

empty jug

Trying to water a field.

Spilled tea

Tea once spilled
Can never quite
Fill the cup
Like it used to.

      There will always be
      Stains on tablecloths,
      Clothes,
      Maybe the floor
      (If you tried hard enough.)

And sometimes
You just have to laugh
And forgive
And appreciate the way
The blotched edges fuzz
And bleed
      And weep
            And feather
                And contain

Like art.
   (not all mistakes are worth crying over).

ive been up
since seven

Boots laced
In stubborn double knots
(I've been up since 7)
Sidewalks paved
With scuffs and fractured cracks
(I walked them all this morning)
I woke up early
By accident
(By choice)
And my mind is bright
And clear.

It is something so magical
To walk past a bush that is chirping
Green arms
Wrapped all in hugs
around a chain-link fence

Please sir
Please
What do the *stones* mean?

sunshine

Sunshine, don't leave me
Warmth, don't go
How can I stay light and soft
Frozen over with ice and snow?

Today is... not good

I dig my nails
Into my skin
Scared I'll rip
I'm paper thin

I'm shattered pieces
(Breathe, release it)

Ice my heart against the burn
Won't move
think
breathe
speak
out of turn

Silent now, I stay in line
Shut down the voice that screams and cries

A gilded cage
A songbird fighting
Against the rhythm undermining

All I hear and all I do
And how I think and when I move
And how I see and what I speak
And what is dark and where is light

And when is day and why is night
And who is wrong and what is right

And through

This song

I fight

The beat is taking over
Sending me to supernova
In a flash of light
To pierce the night
I sway from line
These words are mine

But all of this is in my head
My eyes are dull, my heart is dead
The rhythm so demanding
Leaves me barely strength for standing
My fire fades too fast and
Hark! Those embers' final gasp

this song-

bird breaks

her song.

i was poetic
this morning...

I was poetic this morning
As I walked up the stairs
Words and rhythms
Sung through my head

It was something about heartbeats
The way they lead the feet
And the feet harmonize with their drum
And the stairs bring out the song in us

I had pictures and poetry spurring me on
To paper and a pen to record them
Save them
Mapping my world, my time, my mind

And then I sat down
In my seat, in my class
And my heart remembered how to beat in time
On its own, soft and silent in the background
Operating independently
And leaving my mind free for
More Important Things
After all
What place is there for a heart's beat
When none have time to listen?

Avocado in a sunny windowsill on a warm day in February

The avocado did not ripen on its tree
Not all the way

Not outside
Under the sunlight
& the sky

Not before it was plucked
By the hand of a worker
Packed
In the isolation of a designated spot
In a crate
Crowded, yet alone

Not in the store
Under the harsh fluorescent lighting
So different
So alien
So cold
So unlike the soft warm sun

Not until
It was picked up
Brought to a home
Deposited on a windowsill
And left to soak in the unusual warmth
Of this February day

Now does it ripen
Now is its time.

How to grow up :

How to grow up:
Don't.

Cling to the stars
Gaze up, crane your neck, feel the weight
Your hair in its lopsided ponytail
(No matter what they tell you
nothing decrees that
you must have it perfectly centered
or straight)
Paint your nails—
some, or half, or one, or all—
Whatever your heart desires.
Put art on your fingers
And the toes of your
Bare feet, pressed against slanted ceilings
As the smells of wood fires
Drift through the screen
In, like the breath the world takes
As it wakes, rising in the morning
With gentle blue-toned shadows
And whispers of tires on pavement
Even before the sun

Get up
Early enough to breathe

And don't make your bed
(Unless it will make you happy when you return)

Get dressed
Wear clothes that make you admire yourself
In mirrors, windows, reflections on the train
(It is not vain to love the way you look
nor in vain if it makes
the weight of your heart a bit lighter to bear)

Press your hand to the glass when it rains
And your nose to the pane when it snows
Or better yet
Go out through the door
Hold hands with the universe
Dance to the time of the storm, or
Reach high, clasp palms, and twirl with the sun
Spun in the wind
Whichever the day warrants
(There will be days that warrant one
or the other, or both,
or something else entirely.)

You'll know, so don't worry.
Don't worry about up, that unattainable goal.
Don't grow up. Just grow.

April Showers

April showers bring May flowers
They say, they've said for ages gone
But what when April's dry as bones
Parched and bleached by desert suns
And May, her lover, weeps and groans
And the flowers blossom anyway?

Somedays

Somedays

Somedays
The sunlight is just within reach
And i am too tired to stretch out my arm

i swear like a sailor

I swear like a sailor
Who has never been to sea before
Dancing around the rigging
Scared that I will trip
And expose my ignorance to the world
Scared because
It seems
Everyone else has been sailing all their lives
Or else has planted their roots
Deeply on the land
While I want to see the earth
From sea
Because weren't we given it all?

Always out of reach
Like a top shelf
For one who stopped growing
Far sooner than she wished.
Always out of reach
Like the solution, the
Repair of something broken
Which you didn't mean to drop.
Always out of reach
Like days
When the clouds
Don't grace my mind's sky.
Always out of reach
Like happy
Beyond circumstances.

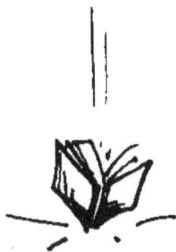

happy beyond circumstances

your wings were meant to soar
not just to shield
as you have become so adept
& achefully accustomed to

— sj blash

death of light

If only I had wings, I would take flight
So far above this murky world which sees
Beauty in the death of light

Often when I walk the streets at night
The wind tears through me, and although I freeze
If only I had wings, I would take flight.
I'd climb the clouds till I was out of sight
Day and night, they're all the same to me.
Beauty in the death of light?
I don't believe that light can truly die
Sunset cues the sunrise somewhere free.
But if only I had wings I would take flight.

I'd marvel at the world from this great height
Look down and spot the mountains, cities, seas
But beauty in the death of light?

If I chased the sun across the sky in all its might
Still futile like a tail I'll never seize
So if only I had wings I would take flight
The beauty is there is no death of light.

Toothpaste
And ripped curtains

I spit
Into the sink
And run my teeth
Under my tongue
and
My toothbrush
Under the faucet
Did I
       I wonder
Scrub them clean
Enough to rid them
Of the grime
Of the day?
Like that cheesy commercial
Which promises
To turn back the clock
Of dental health?
(So it doesn't come back later
To bite me ;)
And I grin
And stick out my tongue
And crinkle my nose
In pride and humor
To my reflection

Which returns the gesture
And the tattered
Communal shower curtains
Shudder
And shriek on their rods in disappointment

And I don't care
Because a smile
Is never a shame.

Red

Red is Mondays,
Swirling in a poisoned cloud
Like the aether
Ready to grab my hand
And throw me into the middle of the week
Before I know
What it is exactly that I have touched
(and before I am ready as well)

Red is apples
Macintosh melancholy
And candle wax gala
Red is an explosion
Of dark magic
Red and black, the perfect duo
Twisting and weaving in their dance
All low notes
And timpani rumbles
And middle C
And like the dueling harmonies
Red is too loud
Too bright
And at the same time
Always present
Always safe.

Red is blood
In the same way my emotions are of pearl
Luminescent and shifting
If you see them,
Something's wrong.

tired

I am tired.
Tired
Tired
Tired.

Muddy brown
        Chocolate cake
Pine-needle green
        Exhausted,

Tired.
Until words of weariness
Are the only ones left in my mind,

Cluttering the floor
        Like peanut shells

When the elephants of social interaction have
passed.

144

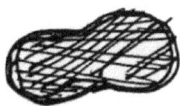

NINE:

another came

trapped

Society may have built the walls
And technology gave me the key
But for trapping my thoughts
In the pit of my soul
I have no one to blame but me.

I turned my chest to a cavity
I scooped out my heart in my palms
I beat at the words till they shattered and fled
Leaving me bloodied and frail an alone
Alone

I turned my gaze to the glow of the screen
Ignoring the sand in my eyes
And when the clock told me
unchangeable truths
I regretted it all and I cried
I poured out my soul on the pages
I emptied my mind of my woes
Not enough, still it says
To be ponderous and sad
If nothing you feel ever shows.

overnight

I was
And continue to be
A fool
To imagine that a single night
Will change things
Rome was not built
In a day
But every time
Every moment
I allow myself to hope
Maybe this time
Change will stick.

(I wrote another poem
On the back of this page)

But *no*,
I want to take this paper
And tear
Once from the binding
Once down the center
Shredding these words which mean
N o t h i n g.
Because that's all I say
Flowey cursive
Jaunting rhymes
Which mean nothing, nothing, nothing at all.
I don't doubt my friends
And I don't think they hate me.
I believe their love
But I have none.
No one in this world could hate me

More than I hate myself.
Sticks and stones and slings and arrows
Do not hurt, I hold the stores
Kindness will disarm me
And thus, I trust it not
Even this, these words on page
Are nothing more than ink, from pen
From navy coated nails
Because I've held the words so long
Their burn has long since cooled
Soothed to lukewarm
In the cavity of my mouth
Un-said.

(this page ends, I feel again)

emptied

We stood on the edge of the stage
In a line
As dust mites
Caught the stage lights
And circled us
As we stood
On the edge
Of the stage
In a line
And the lights
Bathed us in golden halo

Three
Two
One

She said

So three
Two
One

We counted

And then we yelled
A cacophony of words

154

To the yawning ear
Of the empty auditorium
Our fears
Our anxieties
Everything we were scared to say

I don't remember what I yelled
What it was I ended up letting out
(maybe that was the point)
But it was half as much as I wanted
And twice as much as I had ever said before

I could yell for an hour
Till my throat is hoarse
And my mind is ragged
And my fears soar
On the updraft of my breath
And climb to the rafters
Like bats
Shataiki
Waiting
Waiting
Waiting for me
To crumple over the edge
Pitch forward over the side
Because my skin
Once emptied of them
Will have nothing to
Contain

Any longer
And I will deflate

Because my hopes
The things
I have dared to love
Cannot fill the space
The space my demons leave behind
(yet)

It would be
Like trying to fill
An auditorium
With me

      just me.

i wonder sometimes
if i eat too much
when i feel too little
because i cannot stand the *hunger*

another dragon came

but i did not let

myself be destroyed

how long

will I keep finding myself

in only the pieces I've left behind?

TEN:

the fight and the fashioning

Pages and pages
Flick by beneath my pen
These are the stories
Of how I lived

when i was small

When I was small
I crouched in the bottom of the tub
After showers
And coached the pools of water to the drain
Until every drop had gone
Or dried
Sometimes with my fingers
Sometimes with my toes
Dragging digits quietly along the damp,
Rough surface of the floor
And somewhere
Past my youth and childhood
I stopped
I dried off
And left
And i did not realize
I had left this piece of me behind
Until just now
Until i looked down
And saw the way the droplets clung to my toes
Under and between
Pulling me back
To a simpler time
When I tried on towel togas
And shawls
And dresses and wraps and skirts
In front of the mirror

And was so proud of my creations
The next great fashions
I was sure
Hugging my childlike body
In a soft cocoon of cloth
In a time when i was not ashamed
Of the chub around my middle
The way my stomach spills over my jeans
Because I ate too much last night
And the dinner before that
And the lunch two days ago
And did not move enough
And sat
And wasted my time
And—
And I do not feel "badass"
In this too short
Too soft body
Which breaks too easily and often
And now i sit on the edge of the tub and cry
But only for a moment
Just for an instant
Because even now i have places to be
And cannot sit
And play with the water
As if i have all the time in the world

(I make time to write a poem though.)

sadness & simplicity

"Just choose to be happy," people say, "and
it's simple, then you won't be sad."
But there is nothing simple about this sad
This ache which lodges itself in my lungs
Infecting my breaths, curling around my bones
And draping foul smog across my mind
Nothing simple about the voices
Which tear me in half between them
Nothing simple about overcoming, living, thriving
When depression tells me I am worthless
But anxiety screams that I am not allowed to be.
And I am not romanticizing it
But there is such a thing as
An unhealthy codependency
I am afraid of the unknown, the unexperienced
The concept of living without them
But they can't exist without me.

nostalgia

*Pay mind, but do not always heed nostalgia
(especially for things which never were.)*

"true to me"

I've been pretending for so long.
Pretending I was fine
Pretending I was "normal"
Pretending I wasn't drowning inside myself
That now,
Authenticity sometimes feels like acquiescence,
Returning to my roots
Feels like one step forward,
Five steps back,
And asking
(Even for help)
Feels like acting
Because I used to pretend
I could do it on my own.
And the lies which tempt me most
Are the ones that feel the truest.
(Like the one which says
the only one I'm hurting is myself,
if the only one who knows I'm hurting is myself).

So what about when "true to me"
feels like regression?

Who are you?

"Who are you?" she asks me
With her elbows on the counter
Bridging her kingdom to mine
Her eyes see past me, through me
And I stop and I stammer
Because— don't ask me that, I don't know.
How should I know?
I am a fellow traveler with myself
On this long and lonely road
Growing as I go
A sparrow searching for a nest
Because the places that used to fit me
Can't hold the ways I've grown

And when I find it, I'll step through that door
Holding hands with my darkest parts
And if I'm lucky I'll get out before
We burn this whole house down
And as it goes, the bridge of our nose
Will tan, but I'll get sunburnt still;
From wandering through the deserts of my mind
I know that she, that me, is out there too
And just because we haven't found us yet
Doesn't mean we aren't out there to find.

Our paths just haven't crossed since they diverged
In a yellow wood I near forget
Ever since the wood was cut
Tree by tree, to make the walls
That make the bedroom in the hall
Above the stairs where I'm still hiding
All my problems,
hoping I'll be gone before they find them.
That wood which held me as I was torn asunder
The paint which soaked up silent tears for years
Can never feel like home, and is it any wonder
That I've tied the pink and yellow to my fears?

And have I taken the road less traveled
In hopes of finding something new?
Or am I only pressing on in spite
In spite of how I slowly come unraveled and unglued?
Alone and lonely—yes, I am
But why change course? For all I know
I'm almost to some place to rest
And halfway to some sort of home

And she doesn't blink or stammer
Her gaze was glazed, and now confused
Because all along she asked me how
I was; she wasn't asking who.

(And in lieu of that I meant to say
"good thanks, and how are you today?")

girls with doubled knots

We are the girls with doubled knots in our
bootlaces
Sunshine in our smiles
And the stars in our eyes
We who wonder out the windows of the train
And wander just to feel the cities moving
We who under grey skies are outside
Laughing in the snow
Even though
It has soaked through our shoes and dampened our
socks.

Parallel

I wonder how many lives
I have walked across
Not through
Not long enough for them
To learn my face,
My name,
My speech.
Perpendicular
Or perhaps just intersecting at
A single point of intersection
How many of them twice?
Or thrice, or more?
And how many lives
Run parallel to mine?
Destined never to meet
Unless one of us deviates
From our course
(and please, can it be you?)
How many crosswalks
Could have joined our paths
If we had taken them
(And who would the universe
have demanded we trade?)

How many dreams do we enter?
For the brain cannot
Make up or devise a face
Only draw from memories
Long forgotten
When our fingers brushed
As you handed me my fruit
Did an echo of my soul
Splinter off
And bleed into your skin
Like ink
And seep into your dreams?
(is that why I still think of you?)
And if I found you again
Could I have it back?

I am too fragmented already
I have put down roots-
No, not roots
I am a sparrow
Shedding feathers as I
Flit from place to place.
On second thought,
Keep it.
Weave the fluff into
Your nest
If you like
And I will keep going

Dropping feathers
And collecting
A treasure trove of scraps and shinythings
Until I meet another traveling heart
And suddenly
Keeping echoes and ghosts
Are not enough

And we will keep each other, then.

This is not my city

This is not my city.

It is too wide
Too spread out
The bricks are tan
And you can see the sky

The shadows are odd
And I feel little,
A little like a girl in a maze
With the top cut off.

There is so much sun
So much sky
Too few trees and —
Where *are* the telephone lines?

It is not my city
I know this in my heart
But it is beautiful anyway

After all, it belongs to someone
And they call it home.

The wild whispers my name

The wild whispers my name
Softer than I can make out
Louder than I can ignore

Its tendril shoots out
Catching my wrist
As I brush my hand over the blue curtain
Gracing the lightbox window of an Ikea room
(Tragedies in monochrome, these homes
Designed for everyone
But used and loved and lived by none.)

It whispers urgently,
With frantic haste like a childhood friend
Trying to fit all the catching up
Stories and touches and looks
Into suitcases, stuffed over-full already
Every treasure too precious
To consider leaving behind.

It whispers:
"Wrap yourself up in the blue
And let the light swallow you up
Burn the dirt and grime away
You,
Sparrow,
You are a glass prism bird

176

Held aloft against the backdrop of the night
Turning the light of the stars into colors
A rainbow dance
You were forged from them, after all.
Their song is yours.
I will be the hands that hold you up;
The wind which takes you away,
Teaching you to fly.
You have been grounded so long
Darting back and forth to avoid the feet
Things which nearly crushed you.
They did not mean it,
Most of them,
But they could not see you.
They did not see you
And so they thought nothing
Of the crunch under the edge of their shoes.
You did not fault them.
Not when you did not have the words
To inform them of your fragility
Nor the voice to ask if they might mind you
A little more gently, please?

No one told you, did they?
Let me:
Wings are meant to soar
Not to shield
As you have become so adept at
So achefully accustomed to.

You never learned the joys of flight—
Dearheart, won't you let me show you?"

I hear it all
In the texture of this cloth trailing through my
fingertips
Firing the appropriate synapses in my brain.

I hear it all, and my heart thrums
Vibrating with longing
As the stardust shivers with the song in my blood
The song that I was never taught
(The song I am learning, note by note)
But I keep walking
I do not swaddle myself in blue love
The kind of blue the light shines through
And makes alive

I let go
Not ready yet for flight
And all that it might mean

(it might mean there is more to choose from than the
ground.)

how long?

How long can I continue on

Still finding myself

In all the pieces

I thought were lost

behind me?

m a n i a

How am i supposed to sleep
When starlight thrills through my veins
And the clouds obscuring the moon only bring
The music of the rain?
I am barefoot, bare-legged,
Bare arms, bare cheeks,
Hair tied up to bare my neck
as the air brushes kisses gentle and sweet
And these four walls
Are too small
For me to dance until i fall
And the rain speckled grass outside doth call
Begging to wash my feet.
So tell me this will be here when i wake
And goodnight is not goodbye
Its been so long since I've felt so alive
So how am I supposed to sleep?
I feel a stirring deep inside
Like a slumbering child on the bank of a stream
Beginning to toss and roll and stir
In her long kept cage of dreams.
And she hasn't opened her eyes yet
For fear it all shall melt away
But golden hopes like butterflies rise
And she might be ready at last to wake.

infinity

Bare feet
Kiss the earth
Lie on your back
And feel the ground and sky
Surround you on all sides
Rest
Be refreshed,
But don't stay too long
        (When a moment is stretched to infinite
                True infinity turns stale.)

sonnet for a sparrow

One day as I went out upon the earth
I saw a sparrow soar above my head.
She swooped and dove and gave the sun wide berth;
Despite no threat or danger still she sped.

Her wings were sharp and bold against the blue.
She seemed to cut the air where'r she went.
And though no others joined her as she flew
She needed none's approval or dissent.

Eventually she vanished from my eyes,
But stayed she on my mind the whole day long.
My focus strayed to thoughts of far off skies
And even as I worked I heard her song.

And I wished then that like her I could be
Alone with just the wind, the sky, and me.

182

someday

someday
there will be those who come after us
soft boys and tough boys
rough girls and fluff girls
and every shade of other in between
someday
they will sit where we have sat
and talk of what we said
and we will hand our world over to them
and they will take it
this fragile trembling beast
(we called it earth)
and it will be their world
and it will not be the same world
this earth-thing, this legacy
relies on every story
every creature that has ever walked across its skin
and I
for one
will tread lightly
softly
and paint flowers instead of trampling them.

Paris is always a good idea

"Paris
Is always a good idea"

But not always a practical one.

Listening to the rain
Is always a good idea.

But what about when the sun is shining?

Walking
And watching the world turn
Is always a good idea.

But what about
When your bones are heavy
And your limbs
Too weak to hold you up?

To rest
To sleep
Perchance to dream
Is always a good idea.

But what if
There is just too much to do,
Or you close your eyelids

> *And find yourself confronted*
> *With only*
> *The interior of your mind?*

Light

                      Is always a good thing.

Color
Rainbow, grayscale, or monochrome
                      Is always a good thing.

Life
Life lived
(If not always loved)
                      Is always a good thing.

Joy

                      and if not joy

Hope

                      and if not hope

Calm

                      and if not calm

Peace

                      and if not peace

Breath.

Just breathe.

Fear of poets

I worry sometimes
That I will run out of words
And everything I try to build
Will come crashing down around me.

But on days when the air
Smells of woodsmoke and rain,
And the warm pavement kisses my toes
As my bare feet dance around puddles,

I am reassured
That as long as I do not let
The fear of speaking swallow me
(again)

I will never run out of things to say.
And as long as this beautiful world
Keeps turning
I will never run out of ways to say them.

"you can't just..." " " you can't just..." " you can't just..."

you can't just...
"you can't just...
" you can't just..."

"you can't just…"

The words have faded now
I've heard them too many times
From too many lips
Their summation is this:
"You can't just go through life
Claiming your depression
Your anxiety
And expect to get things,
Exceptions,
Special favors."

And every word
Feels like a punch to the gut
Reawakening
The pain of an old wound.
A hit to my cracked,
Shuddering,
Weak-already walls.
Because it feels like you are saying
"help"
instead.
"You can't just ask for help."

The idea is that
You are good

And then they see
They see that you are trying
And so
When you fail
There is grace

But what when all I've done
Is fail?
And not for lack of trying,
Merely,
Lack of the kind of trying
Which shows?

What about the days
When the battle inside of me
Rages so fierce
That it does not make it outside?

What do I do
When I am not allowed
To speak my struggles
And get help?

When anxiety
Sits on my spine
And drags its talons
Claws
Along my ribs
And my shoulders

Bend and buckle
Under the weight of it?

What about the days
When even the monsters fight
Like parents
And I would give anything
To have left the room
Before they started?
Instead I hide
In the corner of my mind
And wish
That I was anywhere but here

As depression weeps
And sobs and moans
And wrings its hands
Over grief that I am worthless
And anxiety screams
That this is unacceptable

(but neither offer a solution).

I have this need
For everything
To be perfect

But sometimes
Things just need
To be left

~~To be left~~
to be.

someday

Someday
We will be legends
Myth
Whispers on the wind
Our names adrift
And drifting
Or
Someone will find them
Us
And they will say
She blazed a way
She carved the path
She was the first to stand
On this unbroken ground
And say:
"I think the future
Would like a garden here."

Happiness is homegrown

I saw a sign the other day,
Which read:
"Happiness is homegrown."

Homegrown.
Where is home?
And what does it look like?

The song of a long overdue rainstorm,
First buds of spring,
And a childhood fear of bees

The whisper of bamboo in a suburban neighborhood,
The descent of whirlycoptor seeds as a storm blows in,
The song of a thunderstorm on the crest of midnight

Blackout poetry in a French novel,
Peeling stickers on a laptop,
And a stubbornly perennial patch of grass

The strength of will to overcome childhood fears,
Beautiful beasts drawn in notebooks,
And the swirl of ink in water

A hug from the wind,
A radio played outside in the summer,
And a single drop of blood
from a finger pricked on a raspberry bush

A jar of coconut oil melting in the sun,
A bird zooming along the ground,
And a beetle struggling to right itself

The words i wish i had spoken
to all the strangers i've crossed paths with
The frustration rolling in waves
off the woman at the bus stop
And the illnesses which lurk on public transportation

Maybe happiness *is* homegrown
I am learning to make this world my home
For however long I live on it
And I am growing happiness
In every corner.

ELEVEN

The flowers need love to grow

Yes. And?

(And so do I.)

Acknowledgements:

My grandmother cried after reading this.

I gave my first proof copy to her,
to read on vacation.
She took it and, when she gave it back,
took me into her room and said:
"i had no idea-
i had no idea
you didn't see yourself as beautiful"
She hugged me, and cried.
Oh, God.

My grandmother cries like my mother.
I have seen my mother cry; caused it more often
than I would like.
I had never seen my grandmother cry.

"i had no idea.
No idea that you didn't see yourself
as beautiful."
Oh, God.

I do, Gramma.
I do see me as beautiful.

I see me as brave and strong and wild and ablaze with
every color never known to man.
But I could not stop there
seeing every flaw
Every way I felt like The Wrong Piece,
Jumbled with a puzzle not designed for.
Or perhaps, cut wrong,
or bent along the way.
I saw every injury I have caused, intentioned or not.
And I held them.
Closer than I had learned to hold love.
Ever reviewing lessons
that only needed to be taught once.

"I will paint flowers, instead of trampling them."
But that used to mean
walking barefoot
On stones and thorny paths instead of grass
(grass, where i might crush dandelions or crickets
under ignorant, unknowing feet)
walking with eyes down,
lest I step without thought
It used to mean
"My worth is the sum of all the good I put out
Weighed against all the hurt I have unwittingly caused.
So I will paint a hundred flowers
For every butterfly effect I cause
Every breeze that fells a leaf in my wake."
I stood on that scale a hundred times a day

197

And memories mocked me more
Than numbers ever have.
Oh, God.

"it sounds so heavy"
My therapist said.
"this weight you put on yourself"
And I bend like a feeble branch
So close to caving in
what if? what if I have put it on myself?
who, then, can permit me to take it off?

(Oh, God.
that has to be me too, doesn't it?)

This book is about me.
All of it.
The bad, but also, the good.

This book is a journey.
A journey in circles, in cycles.
Everything comes in seasons.
Whether I wish they would leave or stay forever.
But I don't want you to leave,
thinking I do not see myself as beautiful.

This book is a journey, the one I've already taken.
I will write another about the home I am building.

Another of all my words, the ones I've found
between the lines of someone else's.
Another about the maps,
futures hung on my wall and calling to me.
Another still, of all the pages
I cast into moving waters,
sent off with prayers that they will find the hearts
who need to hear them.

But this one: This is an archive, annal, chronicle. A
record of where I started, and where it took me.

I am well. I promise.
I am learning to make this world, this skin, my home.
I am planting a garden of happiness,
painting flowers, <u>and</u> tending to
the ones I trampled down inside of me.

After all,

Flowers need water to grow.

And love.

Right.
flowers need love to grow too.

199

And?

oh.
right.
and so do we.

don't forget that.
<3 Sierra
9/28/2019

Enjoyed this book?
Hoping for more by this author?
Please leave a review! Even just a few sentences
helps other people find the book and will also
genuinely make my day. <3

Buy me a chai to keep me writing:
https://ko-fi.com/sjblasko

Find me around the web and say hello!
Etsy: SparrowgirlTreasures
Instagram: @thesongsofsparrow
Hello Poetry: SparrowSoaring
Website: sjblaskocreations.pb.online

About the Author

This book was a labor of love, but it was definitely a labor. SJ Blasko is, quite frankly, too tired of wrestling with the beast to think of anything clever to say about herself.

If you think you need biographical details to learn about the author, go back and read the book again.

index

www.ingramcontent.com/pod-product-compliance
Lightning Source LLC
Chambersburg PA
CBHW022006090426
42741CB00007B/911